STRAIGHT TALKING

Cocaine

Sean Connolly

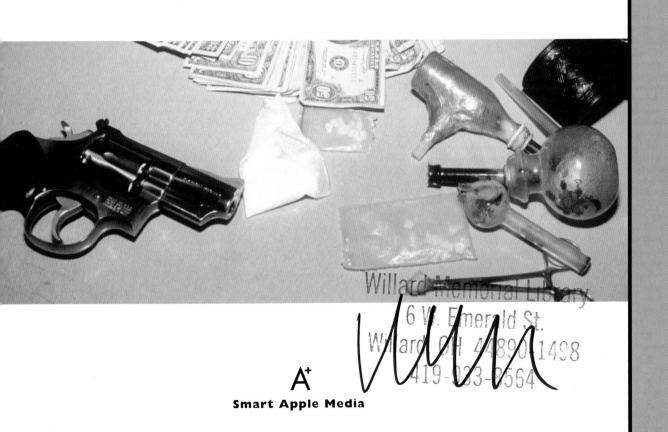

A⁺
Smart Apple Media

Published by Smart Apple Media
2140 Howard Drive West
North Mankato, MN 56003

Designed by Guy Callaby
Edited by Pip Morgan
Artwork by Karen Donnelly
Picture research by Cathy Tatge

Photograph acknowledgements
Photographs by Alamy (Janine Wiedel Photolibrary), Guy Callaby,
Getty Images (Evan Agostini, NICOLAS ASFOURI / AFP, Dave
Benett, John Bradley, Paula Bronstein, John Chiasson / Liaison,
China Photos, Color Day Production, MEREDITH DAVENPORT / AFP,
Paul Edmondson, Britt Erlanson, Andrew Errington, Frank Fisher /
Liaison, Frank Driggs Collection, Yvonne Hemsey, GOH CHAI HIN /
AFP, Dave Hogan / Live 8, Jeremy Horner, Kos, PATRICK KOVARIK /
AFP, John Lamb, David Madison, Erin Patrice O'Brien, Michel Porro
/ Newmakers, Richard Price, STR / AFP, Tony Latham Photography
Ltd., Penny Tweedie, Carlos Villalon / Newsmakers, Gary Villet /
Time & Life Pictures, Ron Wurzer, Elizabeth Young, David Young-
Wolff), The Granger Collection, New York (p. 9)
Front cover photograph by Getty Images (Stewart Bonney
News Agency)

Printed in China

Library of Congress Cataloging-in-Publication Data

Connolly, Sean.
Cocaine / by Sean Connolly.
p. cm. — (Straight talking)
Includes index.
ISBN-13: 987-1-58340-924-4
1. Cocaine abuse. 2. Cocaine. I. Title.

HV5810.C7 2006
613.8'4—dc22   2006001427

First Edition

9 8 7 6 5 4 3 2 1

Contents

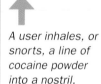

A user inhales, or snorts, a line of cocaine powder into a nostril.

People often drink a cup of coffee or tea first thing in the morning as a pick-me-up. These drinks contain the drug caffeine, which stimulates their body's nervous system and makes them feel more wide awake. Cocaine is a much more powerful, dangerous, and illegal stimulant that some people take—usually in the evening or at night—to help them feel on top of the world for a short time.

Cocaine is becoming more common, so you may meet someone who has the drug—you may even be offered the chance to take some at a private house or at a party. This book explains what cocaine is, what it can do to you, and who takes it and why.

Paying the price

Some people take cocaine because they want to feel a buzz and free themselves briefly from the pressures of everyday life, relationships, or work. Often, they think that cocaine will make them work better or faster. Others take it because their friends or coworkers do, or because they are afraid that they'll seem uncool if they don't.

The sense of pleasure that comes from taking cocaine is brief. It gives people a short boost and makes them feel like they can do—or say—just about anything. But there is a price to pay for this boost. It triggers a desire to take more of the drug as often as possible. Users often either ignore or disregard the negative effects, just as a heavy smoker ignores constant warnings about cancer or heart disease. When people continue to take cocaine, they find it hard to stop, so they develop psychological problems that disturb their health and their relationships with their family, coworkers, and friends. A cocaine habit costs lots of money and often becomes the most important thing in a person's life.

On top of these problems comes the issue of the law. The high-pressure world of drug dealing is a world of crime and potential violence, where producing, selling, possessing, and even passing on cocaine can lead to harsh punishments in many countries.

" I'm 21 years old, and since the age of 16, I have had a massive problem with cocaine. I started out by just taking it on special occasions, but I soon realized that this was a drug that you just couldn't give up. "

Contributor to a Web site for people who have problems with cocaine.

Many people associate cocaine with high living and wild, all-night parties because it is a stimulant that gives a boost of energy.

L ife in the Andes Mountains of South America is hard. Very little rain falls on the steep-sided valleys and the high plains. The air is thin and does not contain as much oxygen as the air at sea level. Farmers work hard to grow crops and make a living from the soil, and then travel long distances across the mountains to take their produce to market. Others work long hours in the appalling conditions and semidarkness of tin and silver mines.

A family wraps up against the cold weather in the Andes Mountains of South America.

GIFT FROM THE GODS

The Inca people believed that coca leaves were sacred—a gift from the gods. During religious ceremonies, Inca priests would chew the leaves and predict coming events or try to cure illnesses. The Inca people also offered coca leaves to their gods in an effort to prevent natural disasters, such as droughts, floods, and earthquakes. They also believed that people's souls would go to paradise if they tasted coca leaves on their deathbed.

About 5,000 years ago, the early inhabitants of the Andes discovered a plant that grew naturally in the mountains and helped them overcome the hardships of life at high altitude. Chewing the leaves of this coca plant relieved their tiredness, hunger, and the constant feeling of cold. At the same time, it boosted their energy so that they could carry on with their tasks.

By 1500 B.C., South American farmers had begun cultivating the plant. Eventually, the coca leaves became sacred and a crucial part of religious rituals. Many people in the mountains of Bolivia, Ecuador, Peru, Colombia, and Chile still chew coca leaves today. Usually, they chew a few leaves for a while to allow the chemicals to seep out, then swallow the juice.

Medical headlines

In the 19th century, European scientists wondered whether the special ingredient contained in coca leaves had a medical use. They successfully extracted cocaine, and as soon as doctors discovered that it shielded people from pain, it made medical headlines. Surgeons and dentists were quick to use cocaine as an anesthetic. Modern medicine uses a variety of safer drugs for this purpose.

Before long, all sorts of medicines and health drinks containing cocaine were advertised in newspapers and appeared in pharmacies. In an age when there were few controls over advertisers' claims, the makers of these products promised buyers extra energy as well as relief from a wide range of illnesses. Respected medical experts seemed to support these claims. For example, the great Austrian psychoanalyst Sigmund Freud believed that cocaine could help people's digestion, make them more alert, and even help cure addictions to alcohol and other drugs.

A 19th-century advertisement shows that people believed cocaine was a cure for toothaches—and safe enough for children.

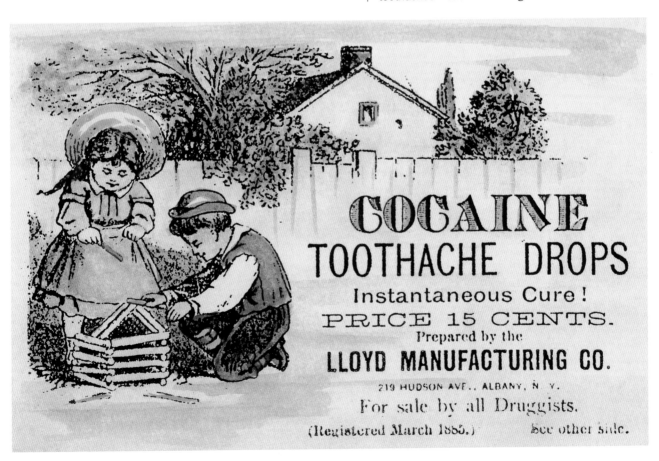

A Colombian farmer sprays his coca plants to protect them against insects and other pests.

A white crystalline powder is made when coca leaves are mixed with other chemicals. Users usually sniff (the slang term is snort) the powder through their nostrils. Addicts may inject a solution of cocaine into their blood. Often, users keep their cocaine in little rectangular packages and refer to it as coke, snow, dust, or toot.

Cocaine sellers often mix, or cut, their cocaine with other white powders, such as chalk, talcum powder, or even laundry detergent.

Sometimes, cocaine is processed even further to produce a drug that can be smoked. This is known as crack.

↑

The form of cocaine known as crack comes in hard chunks, or rocks. The name comes from the process of heating cocaine, which causes a cracking sound.

Understanding the risks

By the early 20th century, cocaine was widely available. People began to notice its side effects and dangers. In particular, it was addictive. Some believed that criminals grew more violent because cocaine boosted their confidence. Dr. Hamilton Wright, an American antidrug activist, wrote that "the habitual use of [cocaine] temporarily raises the power of the criminal to a point where, in resisting arrest, there is no hesitation to murder." Responding to such concerns, the United States government made cocaine use illegal in 1914. In the next few decades, cocaine was made illegal in other countries, too.

New wave of users

Many drugs become popular because of trends among young people. LSD and marijuana first became widely used in the 1960s because they seemed ideally suited to the psychedelic music and dancing of the time. Teenagers would come across these drugs at dances, concerts, and parties. In the same way, ecstasy became the drug linked with the all-night raves of the 1990s. According to evidence collected from 2001 onward by the Home Office in the United Kingdom (UK), cocaine is becoming part of the dance and party scene, alongside—and sometimes replacing—ecstasy. Recent surveys show that 7 percent of people between the ages of 20 and 24 in England and Wales have taken cocaine. This figure is higher than in previous decades.

SEARCHING QUESTION

Many poor South American farmers need to sell coca leaves to survive, even though they are supplying the raw ingredients of the illegal drug cocaine. Should their governments pay them to grow other crops? If so, who should provide the money?

As with other mind-altering drugs, peer pressure is the main reason people take cocaine for the first time. Refusing a drug that has the reputation of being cool or exciting is not easy to do, especially for young people. They are often too embarrassed to say no and don't want to be thought of as boring.

Another reason people try cocaine is curiosity about a drug that is illegal and dangerous. The temptation may be harder to resist when someone reads about musicians, actors, supermodels, and other celebrities who are taking it. If they enjoy chasing the high of cocaine, it's not surprising that young people want to join in the fun and feel better and more talkative—at least for a while. Cocaine may provide a sense of being more alert and clever, and more able to do things that require concentration or thought.

High-earning young office workers are often tempted to take cocaine as part of a lifestyle that involves working hard and playing hard.

Dangerous rewards

The brain contains many powerful chemicals, such as dopamine and serotonin, which stimulate nerve cells and affect behavior. Dopamine, for example, is released when you smell tasty food cooking or when you hear the theme music for a favorite television show.

When cocaine reaches the brain, it triggers the release of dopamine, which creates a rewarding and pleasurable sensation. But the reward is dangerous because it is an illusion. When the effects of the dopamine wear off, the brain may be tricked into needing more cocaine to release the same pleasant sensations. As a result, cocaine users feel the urge to continue taking the drug despite the cost and the risk to their health.

Scientists have shown that this urge exists in experiments on mice, which were encouraged to take cocaine whenever they wanted. The mice continued to take doses of cocaine until they developed heart problems.

The teenage years are hard for those who are not confident in themselves. Peer pressure may lead them to make decisions they later regret.

TAKING COCAINE

Most cocaine is in the form of white powder, which is either loose or in the form of a hard rock. A user usually uses a razor blade or sharp knife to break up the rock or cut the crystals into a fine powder and then sets out several neat rows, or lines, on a clean, smooth surface such as a mirror. The user inhales, or snorts, a line of cocaine quickly into a nostril through a tube, such as a straw or a rolled-up dollar bill.

What users feel

The cocaine is absorbed into the blood through the mucus lining of the nostrils. A feeling of numbness often spreads to the back of the throat. Within minutes, the cocaine reaches the brain. Although no two people have the same experience, most users feel some or all of the following:

- *Excitement and a burst of energy that often involves being very talkative.*

- *Confidence and aggressiveness.*

- *Willingness to take more risks than normal.*

- *An intense desire to take the drug again.*

- *An urge to have sex.*

- *Little or no appetite (some people take cocaine to help with dieting).*

The cocaine high may last no more than about 20 minutes. At the same time, the body temperature rises, the heart rate increases, and the pupils of the eyes grow wider.

Crack

A more powerful form of cocaine, known as crack, is sold in tablets or hard fragments and is smoked in a pipe. A crack high is more intense and almost instantaneous—and it ends after several minutes.

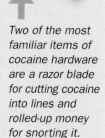

Two of the most familiar items of cocaine hardware are a razor blade for cutting cocaine into lines and rolled-up money for snorting it.

ON TOP OF THE WORLD

During the late 19th century, word began to spread of a drug that could make people feel wonderful. Paolo Mantegazza, an Italian doctor, gave himself a large dose of cocaine and recorded the results. "I sneered at all the mortals," he wrote, "condemned to live in the valley of tears while I, carried on the wings of two leaves of coca, went flying through the spaces of 77,438 worlds, each one more splendid than the one before." It is hardly surprising that people eagerly tried to match his experience.

Exercise can give people a natural high, which is much safer than one brought on by a drug such as cocaine.

A man lights up a pipe containing crack cocaine. The drug will give him a very brief high. Crack smokers often try to smoke another pipe quickly to repeat the high and also to avoid the dismal low that follows.

SEARCHING QUESTION

What sort of person do you think would be attracted to taking cocaine? Would that person also be likely to take other drugs that might make him or her feel differently?

High society

Diego Maradona's soccer career was cut short because of his dependence on cocaine.

For many people, cocaine is linked to the high-living world of big money, fast cars, and expensive yachts.

Cocaine has a reputation as a rich person's drug or an essential part of living in the fast lane—for instance, in advertising, music, or the financial world.

Just being able to afford cocaine gives some people a thrill. It makes them feel like they are enjoying themselves in the same way as rock stars, supermodels, and other high-fliers. It's all part of human nature: other people might get a similar thrill from being able to afford champagne, a sports car, or an expensive yacht.

Forbidden fruit

The link between cocaine and glamorous living goes beyond money. The drug itself, and the high it gives, has been linked to fast-living people for more than a century. The fact that cocaine distorts people's thinking and makes them believe they can do nearly anything makes the drug attractive. But it worried the 19th-century medical scientists who once praised its benefits. As cocaine became illegal in one country after another in the 20th century, it gained a reputation as forbidden fruit.

" Cocaine is God's way of saying you're making too much money. "

Comedian and actor Robin Williams.

An open secret

By the 1920s and 1930s, it was an open secret that some popular singers, songwriters, and other highly paid entertainers were using cocaine. Insiders knew that the unpublished verses of popular songs, such as American songwriter Cole Porter's *I Get a Kick out of You*, referred to cocaine.

Ordinary people, going about their daily lives, picked up the references to snow, cokeheads, and white powder in other popular songs. Noel Coward, the UK's most popular playwright of that period (and someone known for his rich and famous friends), made cocaine one of the features of his play *The Vortex*, set among the wealthy. To audiences, it seemed that cocaine must be another part of high society, just like fur coats, cocktails, and fast cars.

Cocaine was commonly used by the jazz musicians of the 1930s who played at the Cotton Club, a popular nightclub in New York.

Pete Doherty's crack cocaine habit led to the breakup of the Libertines.

COCAINE AND MUSIC

Cocaine has been linked with high-living musicians for almost a century, and in the 21st century, stars continue to take it. One reason cocaine use increased greatly in the 1970s was that famous rock stars sang about—and made no secret about taking—the drug. Legendary guitarist Eric Clapton had a hit record called *Cocaine,* and cocaine played an essential part in the nonstop partying of the rock band Aerosmith. Interviewed in the 1990s, Aerosmith members (who no longer took it) estimated that they had spent millions of dollars on cocaine.

In 2004, Robbie Williams admitted that he had become addicted to cocaine, alcohol, and ecstasy after leaving the British boy band Take That in 1995. He added that Sir Elton John kidnapped him and sent him for treatment in 2000 and that he no longer needed these drugs.

But while one star was on the way up, another was on the way down. Singer Pete Doherty was fired by fellow members of the popular British band the Libertines (which he had begun) because he refused to quit taking cocaine and other drugs. Doherty has tried to rebuild his career without drugs and with the help of his girlfriend Kate Moss (see page 35).

Anyone who produces, sells, or takes cocaine is committing a crime. Why, when cocaine has been illegal for decades, does trade in the drug continue to thrive? The answer is simple: cocaine can make people a lot of money.

Big money

To understand why someone might feel tempted to sell cocaine, you need to think about how much it costs. Cocaine is sold by the gram. Prices vary from city to city and go up and down over time (depending on how much is available), but in 2002 a gram (0.04 oz.) of cocaine sold for between $25 and $150 in the U.S. A gram (0.04 oz.) of any powder is not very much—a typical cake, for example, contains about 200 grams (7 oz.) of flour. So even a small amount of cocaine powder could be worth thousands of dollars.

Much of the world's cocaine is produced in small labs like this one in the forests of Colombia, where a single person can process up to 375 pounds (170 kg) of coca leaves a day.

Cocaine barons

More than three-quarters of the world's cocaine comes from Peru and Colombia, where the coca plants are grown and the leaves processed into cocaine. This part of South America has the right climate to grow coca plants as well as vast areas of wilderness where powerful drug barons have built secret laboratories and transport centers for cocaine.

Colombia's history of political unrest has made it difficult for law enforcement officers to crack down on the barons. As a result, the barons rule successful empires that export cocaine to most parts of the world.

Buyers test cocaine at a secret location in the Caqueta department of Colombia, near the border with Peru and Ecuador. Producers bring their cocaine to such locations every weekend. The cocaine is heated, tested, and then paid for in cash.

A customs officer and his drug-sniffing dog check boxes for drugs. Some breeds of dogs can be trained to bark when they detect even the slightest smell of cocaine.

SEARCHING QUESTION
What kind of punishment do you think drug dealers should receive if they are found guilty? Would the cocaine trade slow down if individual users received the same harsh punishments?

ONE LEAF'S JOURNEY

This is the story of the journey of a single coca leaf on its way to becoming cocaine for sale in New York. A poor farmer in the highlands of Colombia picks the leaf and adds it to the rest of his harvest. An armed enforcer working for a drug baron pays the farmer a very small amount and takes the coca leaves away in a jeep or helicopter. The leaves go next to a heavily guarded secret laboratory, where they are processed into a white powder. This powder is packed into plastic bags weighing no more than two pounds (1 kg).

The bags are packed into a light plane, which flies at night to a Caribbean island, such as Trinidad or Jamaica, where a powerful drug dealer hands over thousands of dollars for the shipment. The dealer promises to pay a passenger (usually a young woman) to fly to New York with cocaine in her luggage. Some passengers wrap the cocaine in small bags and swallow them. They hope to fish the bags out of the toilet when they reach New York.

Reaching New York

Once through customs, the carrier goes to an arranged meeting place and hands over the cocaine in return for a small fee. Dealers take the cocaine to a secret location, where they divide it into small bags containing 10 to 50 grams (0.4–1.75 oz.). When word goes out through text messages that a shipment has arrived, local dealers buy some of the cocaine at a rendezvous and then sell it to the final customer—the user—on a dark street or in a bar.

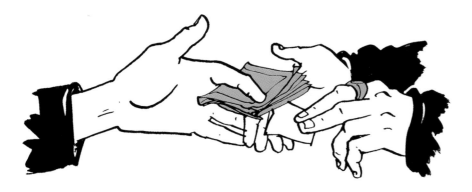

The English language is full of expressions such as "you can't have your cake and eat it too" and "there's no such thing as a free lunch." They are different ways of saying that there is always a price to pay for what we do. In the case of cocaine, that price can be expressed in another saying: "what goes up must come down."

In fact, coming down often describes the feeling people have when the effects of a drug wear off. Very often, the "down" more than matches the "high" they felt not long before. There is definitely a price to pay for the artificial boost that cocaine gives. Payback begins immediately after the effects of the cocaine high have worn off. It may also come much later if the person is a regular user.

Vomiting in a toilet is one possible way of coming down after the high of cocaine.

In the short term

Cocaine can start causing trouble as soon as someone takes it. Someone who takes a high dose or is particularly sensitive to the drug can feel very agitated, aggressive, and even paranoid. The physical side effects caused by the drug include dizziness, hallucinations, vomiting, uncontrolled shaking, headache, and heart pain.

Coming down off the drug triggers another set of side effects in both body and mind. The sense of excitement is replaced with depression, while some of the less pleasant physical effects remain. These include a runny nose, dry mouth, sweating, and loss of appetite.

Problems over time

Most short-term problems caused by cocaine fade if there is a long enough gap between when it is taken. Some heart-related problems, though, can become permanent. Feeling down, anxious, or even paranoid can sometimes become a constant part of a cocaine user's mind.

Even the way people take the drug can cause various problems. Constant snorting of cocaine leads to a permanently runny nose. Over time, the inside of the nose itself becomes damaged—in some extreme cases, the tissue between the two nostrils is worn away. Injecting cocaine leads to a risk of damaged blood vessels and blood poisoning, or developing serious illnesses such as hepatitis and HIV.

The cocaine habit of British TV star Daniella Westbrook led her to attempt suicide and severely damaged the tissue of her nose.

DEATH OF A CHAMPION

The world of sports has been damaged by stories of leading individuals taking drugs, either for recreation or to improve performance. Cycling, one of the most demanding of all sports, is often in the spotlight. In big races such as the Tour de France, cyclists ride as far as 155 miles (250 km) every day for 3 weeks, over mountains, through rain, or in baking heat.

Marco Pantani

Perhaps the saddest cycling story concerns one of the sport's most popular champions. Italian cyclist Marco Pantani had a magical way of riding up mountains, leaving his rivals gasping as he danced on the pedals to the finish line. This skill enabled him to win two of cycling's greatest events, the Giro d'Italia and the Tour de France, in 1998. But many people suspected he had used drugs to succeed.

Pantani became depressed when he retired from the sport, and on February 14, 2004, was found dead in a hotel room in Italy. Giuseppe Fortuni, the coroner in charge of the case, discovered large amounts of fluid in the cyclist's head and lungs. He concluded that Pantani had died of acute cocaine poisoning.

Champion cyclist Marco Pantani developed a costly and deadly cocaine habit after he left the sport in 2003.

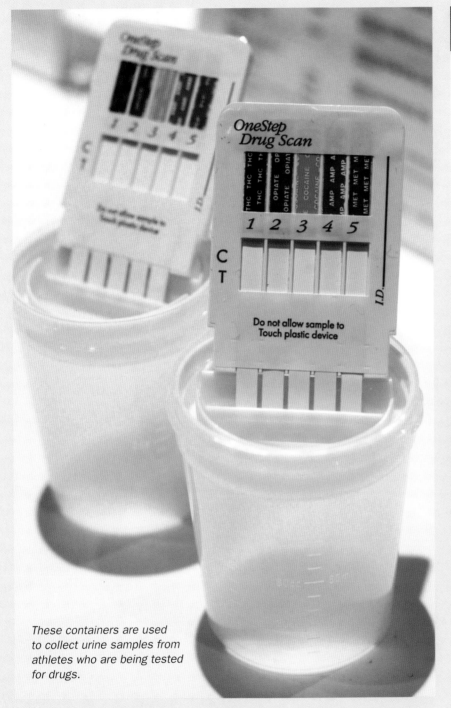

These containers are used to collect urine samples from athletes who are being tested for drugs.

Emergency rooms in U.S. hospitals report illegal drugs when they find them in the blood of a patient. Cocaine is the drug they discover most often.

SEARCHING QUESTION

Imagine that someone you know has had a bad reaction to cocaine. You call the paramedics, but then you face a choice when the ambulance arrives. Should you be honest about what led to your friend's condition (which would help with immediate treatment), or should you cover for him or her by not mentioning the cocaine?

The terms addict, addiction, dependent user, and dependence frequently come up in discussions of nearly every recreational drug, especially cocaine. They all describe an uncontrollable urge to continue using a drug—especially when people know they should not. You may know someone who has become addicted to a drug. For example, most of us know people who are trying to stop smoking or who are worried about the amount of alcohol they drink. These people are battling the urge to continue taking a particular drug—either nicotine (the drug in tobacco) or alcohol.

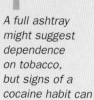

A full ashtray might suggest dependence on tobacco, but signs of a cocaine habit can be harder to spot.

The pull of addiction

The urge to take a drug such as cocaine is not unlike the urge to continue addictive, though less dangerous, behavior. For example, imagine someone who continues playing a computer game after his parents call him to a meal or to get ready for school. He knows he should stop, but the exciting pull of the game makes him ignore these calls, even though he knows he might get into trouble. Even winning the game might not be enough to make him stop—he will start over again, hoping to beat his best score.

Cocaine dependence

The word dependence is more commonly used than addiction to describe the pull a drug has on users. Dependence, which can be physical and psychological, develops after a person has taken a drug over a period of time. Cocaine creates a psychological dependence but not the kind of physical dependence of drugs such as alcohol and heroin.

The pleasurable memories linked to cocaine linger in a person's mind and develop into cravings as soon as the brief cocaine high has ended. They can also develop long after someone has stopped taking cocaine—making it very easy to return to taking the drug after quitting.

 By the time I was 23, I was addicted [to cocaine], but it didn't seem to matter in our business. No one thought it was unusual to be up all night doing lines of cocaine.

Alan McGee, head of Creation Records, quoted in *The Little Book of Cocaine*.

People who are dependent on cocaine need to take the drug so that they can mix with others in social situations.

The power of crack

Crack gives a heightened version of the sensations caused by cocaine powder. The high is higher and briefer, but the fears and anxieties are more obvious, like a speeded-up film of an event. The same is true of crack's ability to make users dependent—they want the drug more and more. They will do anything—even rob and steal—to get it.

One crack user described the powerful urges: "The first hit is always the best. . . . I've never had anything like it. With crack, once you've got that hit of the day, no matter how much you take, you don't get it back. If the rock is there, I can't leave it, even though I don't get anything off it. But you can't just have one [rock] and leave it; you've got to have more."

The extra strain that cocaine places on the heart would seriously harm one of these rowers, who is already making his heart work hard.

COCAINE WITHDRAWAL

The way dependent people react when they stop taking a drug is called withdrawal. There are three main phases of withdrawal.

Phase 1: the crash
Symptoms during the first two to four days include:
- agitation ● depression ● intense craving for the drug ● extreme fatigue

Phase 2: withdrawal
Symptoms during the next 10 weeks include:
- depression ● lack of energy
- anxiety ● intense craving
- angry outbursts

Phase 3: extinction
There is no time limit to this last phase. The temptation to return to cocaine will always be there, especially if the drug is available. It is a time to battle and overcome strong cravings.

SEARCHING QUESTION
Have you ever been so attracted to doing something that you continued doing it even though you knew it was wrong? Can you imagine what it would be like to feel 100 times more drawn to such an activity—would you have the willpower to stop doing it?

Regular cocaine use can cause all sorts of problems—and not just serious medical and psychological concerns. Like any secret habit, regular drug use disrupts everday life and causes conflicts with family and friends. The cost in money is one major reason for these problems. People beg, borrow, and steal to fuel their cocaine habit, and only the very rich do not have to worry about finding the money. Many people run up huge debts, and others turn to crime.

Family members are the best people to help a cocaine user, but very often they find out too late to keep the habit from becoming an addiction. They are left to pick up the pieces by paying for legal costs, supporting a family (if the user has lost his or her job, which is common), or simply trying to help the cocaine user understand how serious things have become. Every story is different, but without honesty and willingness to address the problem, every one is destined to have an unhappy ending.

A cocaine habit puts a lot of strain on other people as well, sometimes stretching families to the breaking point.

WHEN THE MIGHTY FALL

A cocaine habit can destroy a reputation. Dr. Timothy Watson Munro became one of Australia's most famous forensic psychologists in the 1990s. He was a familiar face in Australian courtrooms and on TV when he explained the minds of people accused of serious crimes.

By the late 1990s, Munro was treating wealthy young people with drug problems. What he kept secret was that he was also developing a serious cocaine addiction, which was costing him thousands of dollars a week. In 1999, as part of a wide-ranging drug operation, Melbourne police taped telephone calls in which he was heard ordering cocaine and, in one instance, actually snorting the drug.

Paying the price

In December 1999, Munro gave himself up to police after hearing about the arrest of Andrew Fraser, one of the others involved in the taped telephone calls. He confessed to possessing and taking cocaine. His confession told the story of an energetic and successful public figure reduced to satisfying his daily cocaine habit.

Bruce Cottrill, the judge who heard the case, believed that Munro had already paid a high price in having his drug habit exposed. Some Australians complained that his punishment—a $1,000 fine and a 12-month good behavior bond—was not harsh enough. But most people agreed with the judge, knowing that Munro would be paying the price for many years to come.

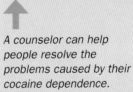

A counselor can help people resolve the problems caused by their cocaine dependence.

COUNTING THE COST

The issue of money is never far from any discussion of cocaine. Despite a significant drop in price since 2004, the drug is seriously expensive. In early 2005, The London Observer newspaper reported that a regular user will spend almost $300 a month on cocaine. Crack addicts spend more than two and a half times that amount—about the same as heroin addicts.

RECOGNIZING THE PROBLEM . . .

Even if you have never seen someone taking cocaine, it is important to recognize the effects of an overdose. Somazone, a Web site promoting drug awareness among young people, lists some of the most common signs of an overdose:

- *No response to shaking, yelling, or pinching.*
- *Shallow breathing or none at all.*
- *Slow pulse or no pulse at all.*
- *Blue lips, toenails, or fingernails.*
- *Snoring or breathing that has a gurgly sound while sleeping or dozing.*

Take action if you find someone with these symptoms.

. . . AND TAKING EMERGENCY ACTION

Becoming unconscious after taking cocaine can be very serious. Lifebytes, another Web site for young people, outlines the following steps you should take if you find someone unconscious, for whatever reason:

- *Place the person on his or her side to prevent choking if he or she vomits.*
- *Call an ambulance as soon as possible with the address ready at hand.*

- *Check the person's breathing—be prepared to do mouth-to-mouth resuscitation or to take any other action that the operator might advise.*
- *Keep the person warm but not too hot.*
- *Stay with the person at all times.*
- *If you know what has been taken, be honest and tell the ambulance crew. If you have a sample of the drug, give it to the ambulance crew.*

> ## " I'm going to die young. I just can't stop destroying myself. "

Comedian John Belushi, shortly before his fatal overdose of cocaine and heroin in 1991.

> ## " It makes you feel great and powerful and all that. The trouble is, it can make you really wired. And it doesn't last that long, so the temptation is to have another line. That's why I found it so addictive, and it cost me a fortune. "

Regular cocaine user quoted on Drugscope Web site.

NO ESCAPE?

Kate Moss, a supermodel with multimillion-dollar contracts, spent the last months of 2005 in the spotlight because of her cocaine habit. Rumors that she took cocaine had been common but unproved. Then, in September, a British newspaper published a photo of her snorting cocaine with boyfriend Pete Doherty (see page 19) in the background. She admitted her cocaine use publicly, but her apology was not enough to save her modeling contracts with H&M and Burberry clothing or with the French fashion company Chanel.

If laws alone could control every wrong or dangerous activity, the world might be safer. Would-be criminals might consider the likely punishment for their actions—heavy fines or long prison sentences—and decide that the risk was not worth taking. But crime does exist, and people are convicted of murder, assault, robbery, and other offenses. The public and the government understand this harsh truth and try to find ways of combatting crime.

Some ways are traditional. Parents encourage decency and honesty in their children, which is reinforced by schools and churches. Educational messages discourage the use of drugs and highlight the risks of taking them. Neighbors band together to keep an eye on each other's homes and property, deterring potential robbers. Prisoners serving sentences are encouraged to build new, honest skills for the time when they return to the wider world.

Drug offenses are relatively new crimes, but the same broad approach can help to deal with them. Many countries have clearly stated laws against dealing and possessing cocaine and other drugs. These are backed up with enforcement and punishments that aim to protect individuals and society from the dangers of drugs.

This young man is lucky to be in therapy to help overcome his cocaine habit before it leads to harm or trouble with the law.

Dinner party targets

Some rich and powerful people believe that their money or influence can prevent them from being convicted of crimes. People at fashionable dinner parties often take cocaine openly, confident that they won't have to pay the price for their actions.

Law enforcement officials are beginning to target these users. On February 1, 2005, Sir Ian Blair was appointed head of London's Metropolitan Police, the most important law enforcement position in the UK. On his first day, he promised to devote police time and money to tracking down these cocaine users. The new police policy is part of a tough campaign to demonstrate that no one is above the law.

Passing cocaine among friends, according to British law, is the same as supplying the drug and carries harsh penalties for those convicted of it.

The Chinese government is strongly against drug abuse but is also determined to educate the Chinese people about the risks.

" *I'm not interested in what harm it is doing to them personally. But the price of that cocaine is misery on the streets of London and blood on the roads of Colombia and Afghanistan.* **"**

Sir Ian Blair, head of London's Metropolitan Police, explaining his reasons for targeting dinner party cocaine users.

OPPOSITE APPROACHES

There is a growing debate about the best way to deal with the threat of cocaine and other drugs. On one hand, many people argue that existing laws should be strengthened and more heavily enforced. The U.S. classifies cocaine as a Schedule II drug, and it is illegal to produce, supply, or possess it, except for medical purposes. Laws in the UK also make it illegal to possess, use, make, or sell cocaine.

On the other hand, some people believe that drugs should be legalized like alcohol and tobacco so that users would be sure of buying real cocaine instead of a mixture of mysterious (and possibly fatal) white substances. UK supporters of legalizing drugs say that the government could earn more than $10 billion a year by taxing them. The extra money could be used to educate people about the dangers of drugs, just as the government now pays for programs to control smoking and alcohol abuse.

Straight talking and strong family bonds can be part of any household. Good communication and an open attitude make it easier for a family to discuss serious issues such as drugs.

THE DUTCH EXPERIMENT

Since the 1970s, the Netherlands has had a unique drug policy. Drugs such as cocaine and heroin are not legal, but users are helped while police target the producers and sellers. Drug users receive less punishment than in many other countries and are encouraged to enter drug awareness programs.

Addicts receive clean needles and substitute drugs. Evidence suggests that this approach helps steer people away from regular drug use. The number of Dutch teenagers who have taken cocaine is among the highest in the world, but the number who regularly take it is very low compared with other European countries.

SEARCHING QUESTION

Governments could earn large amounts of money by taxing drugs if they were legalized. Do you think this would be a good reason to legalize cocaine, especially if most of the money was spent on drug awareness, prevention, and rehabilitation?

Developing a cocaine habit is often a frightening experience. As people spend more time (and money) finding the next batch of the drug, they spend less time with the very people who could help them deal with their problem. Teenagers often find it hard to talk to their parents and other family members. Hiding a drug problem makes them even less willing to discuss things. Friends who are not regular cocaine users are often ignored, either because the user feels they would not understand the problem or because they have drifted apart anyway.

Local help

Admitting they need help is the one of the hardest steps users have to take in the process of becoming free of cocaine. Drugs are hardly a new problem. Some adults have experienced the same problems and choices that young people face, and most of them know where to turn for help.

Young people should approach adults they trust—teachers, youth group leaders, or even the police—for information and advice on cocaine. Many are trained to help young people connect with counselors or drug programs.

A counselor can help cocaine users face their needs, making it easier for them to find out why they take the drug and how they can stop.

COMMUNITY ACTION

People in neighborhoods affected by drugs often live in fear—for their children or for their property and safety. One such area is King's Cross, part of the borough of Camden in central London. Here, there is widespread drug abuse and violent crime linked to crack cocaine.

Prompted by a story about their neighborhood in the *Evening Standard* newspaper, King's Cross residents have set up a Web site to publicize their problems—and to call for stricter controls on drugs.

John Messiter, a teacher living in the neighborhood, organized the Web site and posted photographs he had taken secretly to make it easier for police and drug officials to track down the criminals. These photographs show drug deals taking place and users actually taking drugs.

A drug deal on a city street. Residents of many urban neighborhoods are taking action to reclaim their streets from drug-related crimes.

LOOKING OUTWARD

Australia has a population scattered over a vast area and has been a leader in developing ways of linking individuals and communities. Australians were among the first to use Web sites to spread information throughout their country. Many Web sites offer drug information and treatment advice, as well as links to more specialized information and services.

The Helping Hands Web site, organized by the Australian government, is ideal for young people who are looking for information about cocaine and other drugs. The Web site of the U.S. National Institute on Drug Abuse offers a similar first step.

Many drug-related Web sites contain true stories sent in by young people who have struggled with cocaine and other drug problems. Reading their accounts can help a person understand more about the problem.

Surfing the Internet has allowed many people to make contact with others who share the same fears and concerns about cocaine— sometimes in other countries.

Group programs

Special programs concentrate on helping young drug users change their way of thinking—away from taking cocaine and toward living a fuller life. One such program is the Fitzroy Day Program in Melbourne, Australia. It focuses on young drug users between the ages of 12 and 21.

The Fitzroy approach, which is used in other successful drug programs, encourages young people to learn and develop skills, and helps them forge a sense of shared purpose with others who have had similar experiences. It also helps them understand that it is important to be able to get along with other people and the wider world beyond. The participants take part in group activities that often concentrate on helping the environment, rather than looking only inward and seeking a short-term buzz.

A hug or an understanding word from another person is sometimes all it takes for troubled cocaine users to find the strength to battle their drug problem.

❝ Why, oh why, is the government housing [crack addicts] among the elderly, the vulnerable, or anyone else for that matter, in normal public housing? They should be in monitored institutions, where they should be forced to undergo treatment. ❞

From a personal story submitted to the Crack Cocaine in Camden Web site (www.crackcocaineincamden.co.uk).

SEARCHING QUESTION

What do you think of the suggestion made by the Camden resident quoted above?

acute extreme

addiction the overpowering physical or mental need to do something

affliction the cause of physical or mental pain

amphetamines drugs that work on the body's nervous system to lift a person's mood

anesthetic a drug or other medicine used to reduce the feeling of pain

bond a written legal promise to do something

cultivating growing for harvest

dilated wider than normal

drug barons powerful criminals who control the production and sale of drugs, especially those coming from South America

ecstasy an illegal drug that lifts a user's mood for several hours

exhilaration an intense feeling of cheerfulness

fatal causing death

forensic psychologist a medical specialist who helps in courts or in police investigations

hallucination a sensation of something that does not exist outside the mind—for example, imagined sights or sounds

heart attack damage to the heart when it is deprived of oxygen

hepatitis a disease that enlarges the liver and causes a high fever

HIV an abbreviation for human immunodeficiency virus, which can lead to the deadly condition acquired immune deficiency syndrome (AIDS)

narrate to tell a story

originate to come from

overdose too much of a drug for the body to absorb safely, leading to serious health problems and even death

paranoid believing (because of a mental condition) that the outside world is hostile

peer pressure persuasion from people your own age to do something in order to remain part of the group

peers people of a similar age or social group

psychoanalyst a specialist who uses psychological skills and training to study people's behavior

psychological relating to the mind and how it operates

psychosis a mental condition that leads a person to lose contact with reality

rehabilitation a supervised return to good health

stimulants drugs that affect the nervous system and make a person feel more energetic and lively

stimulate to make something react more strongly

stroke a blockage of a blood vessel leading to the brain, causing difficulties in speaking and moving; in severe cases, it affects thinking and may even cause death

Books

Barter, James. *Cocaine and Crack*. San Diego: Lucent Books, 2002.

Karch, Steven. *A Brief History of Cocaine*. Boca Raton, Fla.: CRC Press, 1998.

Kittleson, Mark, ed. *The Truth about Drugs*. New York: Facts on File, 2005.

Kuhn, Cynthia. Buzzed: *The Straight Facts about the Most Used and Abused Drugs from Alcohol to Ecstasy*. New York: W.W. Norton, 1998.

Manley, Claudia. *Crack and Your Circulatory System: The Incredibly Disgusting Story*. New York: Rosen Central, 2001.

Palenque, Stephanie Maher. *Crack & Cocaine=Busted!* Berkeley Heights, N.J.: Enslow, 2005.

Wagner, Heather Lehr. *Cocaine*. Philadelphia: Chelsea House, 2003.

Web sites

Drug Addiction Crisis and Referral Hotline
www.drug-addiction-hotline.com/cocaine.html
Provides information about drug addiction and how to get help.

Drug Enforcement Administration
www.usdoj.gov/dea
Home page of the U.S. agency in charge of drug enforcement. Contains drug use statistics and information on law enforcement.

Drug-Rehabs.org
www.drug-rehabs.org/faqs/FAQ-cocaine.php
Provides referrals to drug treatment centers throughout the United States.

Focus Adolescent Services
www.focusas.com/Cocaine.html
Offers cocaine treatment options and referrals for teen addicts.

Helping Hands
www.drugs.health.gov.au/youth/helping_hands/index.htm
An ideal place to start investigating cocaine and other drugs.

Index